Woldemar Kaden

The Baths of St. Moritz

Woldemar Kaden

The Baths of St. Moritz

ISBN/EAN: 9783741122507

Manufactured in Europe, USA, Canada, Australia, Japa

Cover: Foto ©Lupo / pixelio.de

Manufactured and distributed by brebook publishing software
(www.brebook.com)

Woldemar Kaden

The Baths of St. Moritz

THE
BATHS OF ST. MORITZ.

THE LEADING HEALTH-RESORT
OF THE UPPER ENGADINE.

By

WOLDEMAR KADEN.

"An *Acetosum fontale* which I prize
above all that I have met with in
Europe is in the Engadine, at St. Moritz;
the same runneth sourest in the month
of August. He who hath drunk of
this same drink as of a medicine, he
can talk of health."

Paracelsus. (A. D. 1530.)

ZURICH
O'RELL FÜSSLI & Co.
1886

*   *   *

Stern are thy looks, my Engadine,
In highland airs a throne is found thee;
White is thy head, the Piz Bernin',
And glaciers form a girdle round thee.
But seldom sounds the song of birds,
Of roses thou art not the home,
And even in thy children's words
I hear the raging torrent foam . . .

And yet in beauties thou'rt array'd,
At even, when thy peaks are glowing,
When in the quiet larch-woods' shade
The thousand Alpine flow'rs are blowing.
The wavelets of a rushing stream
Thy emerald lakes with splendour fill;
With healing springs thy mountains teem,
Assuaging many a human ill . . .

*   *   *

THE ENGADINE.

CHRISTOPHER COLUMBUS discovered America towards the close of the fifteenth century, but the "discovery" of Switzerland dates from a much later period. Strange and paradoxical as this statement may appear to some persons, it is nevertheless true that Switzerland *as* Switzerland, namely as a land of sublime and magnificent scenery, the favourite resort of every admirer of the beauties of nature, was discovered no earlier than the eighteenth century. And even then its manifold charms were revealed only by slow degrees, for the finest of its valleys, the Engadine, remained long after, for many, many years, a *terra incognita*.

Attention was first drawn to Swiss scenery through the publication in the year 1729 of a poem entitled "The Alps", written by the celebrated physiologist Haller. He was the earliest pioneer on the paths leading to the grandest scenery of which Europe can boast, but it was not long before many others began to follow where he led. Thirty years later Jean Jacques Rousseau, in his romance "La nouvelle Héloïse", celebrated the enjoyment of nature as the purest of delights. The signal given by Rousseau was at once responded to by the entire cultured world, eager to escape from the monotony which then pervaded society, and sentimental souls flocked to the west of Switzerland to satisfy their yearnings on the lovely shores of Lake Leman.

But the rest of Switzerland still awaited its path-finder, The entire district of the High Alps, the domain of ice-crowned peaks, glaciers, snowfields, and sequestered valleys was still enveloped in an impenetrable mist; of all this territory and its inhabitants little was known beyond more or less vague and uncertain traditions: on its horizon neither Murray nor Bædeker had begun to dawn.

But in the fulness of time two new explorers arose, Saussure and J. G. Ebel. In his "Voyages dans les Alpes" Saussure, a celebrated Genevese savant, lifted the veil from the district of the High Alps; while the numerous explorations and discoveries of the German physician and natural philosopher Ebel withdrew it from the more secluded parts of Switzerland. Thousands upon thousands now came from all quarters of the globe to admire the wonderful and magnificent features which Nature here exhibits to mankind. Then too it was that the German poet Schiller poured forth his impassioned song of freedom, his drama of "Wilhelm Tell", and aroused in the hearts of all his readers an enthusiasm for the home of the hero whose deeds he sung.

The era of secular pilgrimages was now inaugurated. Switzerland had become the Mecca of every lover of nature, and all were impatient to see its verdant pastures, its glassy lakes, its sky-piercing peaks. In the course of time the fame of the beauties of the little land penetrated into the remotest climes, and poets and painters were the zealous apostles of this evangel.

All were now eager to contemplate these sublime landscapes, and to renew the vigour of their minds at this fount of high enjoyments; and soon too it was discovered that the Alpine air was potent to cleanse, as with a stream of crystal water, lungs clogged with the dust and the noisome exhalations of crowded cities.

An occasional visit to Switzerland was now no longer a mere matter of fashion; to many it had become a necessity, and the shrewd and industrious inhabitants of the country no sooner perceived this than they applied themselves with energy to secure the promised harvest. Hundreds of hotels of more or less pretension sprang up like mushrooms at all points, old roads were improved and new ones constructed, railways were laid through the valleys, and steamboats were launched on the lakes. Everything was done to make things easy for the traveller, and every stumbling-block was removed out of his way. Now also the numerous medicinal springs began to receive attention.

And our Engadine?

Back yonder, where Piz Bernina lifts his snowy crest to a height of more than 13,000 feet, lording it proudly over the surrounding peaks, where the River Inn flows swiftly through a triad of crystal lakes, where the glittering ice-fields of Morteratsch and Roseg hang high above the green valleys, — there the tranquillity of centuries was still unbroken. As yet there was no highway leading into the Engadine, and not an invalid crossed the mountain-barrier to quaff health-giving draughts at the most powerful medicinal springs of Europe.

That was forty years ago.

Great and noteworthy was the change that all at once took place. The people of the Engadine suddenly began to bestir themselves, and henceforth they knew no more rest; at the present day they are little disposed to subside into inactivity. By dint of digging and delving, excavating, blasting, filling in, levelling, and embanking, they have with their own hands constructed secure and magnificent highways, perfect masterpieces of the engineer's art.

And why?

The outer world had suddenly recognised the beauties of the Engadine; invalids restored to health had made known the sanative powers of its mineral springs. The epicures of scenery had saved the Engadine to the last as the choicest morsel, and now came to enjoy it; and they were accompanied by many whose health needed recuperating. Thus it is that the Engadine has become the chosen resort of invalids who seek in the waters of St. Moritz relief from their ailments, while its peaks and upland valleys are the El Dorado of mountaineers and admirers of picturesque scenery. The Engadine has now indeed become an important factor in the life of many members of the wealthy classes of England and America, and we feel assured that it is destined to remain so, for at least the Baths of St. Moritz, its principal resort, do not owe their popularity to a mere passing freak of fashion.

The question why the chalybeate springs on the Rosatsch attract such crowds of sufferers is therefore easily answered: The results attained are strikingly favourable, and are manifest to the world.

It is more difficult to account off-hand for the constant increase in the number of tourists and sightseers; for the Bernese Oberland with its stupendous mountains and beetling precipices, its romantic valleys and picturesque waterfalls, or the landscapes of the Lake of Lucerne, the pleasant shores of whose northern inlets are clothed with an almost Italian vegetation, are decidedly more beautiful (as beauty is commonly understood), are more interesting and attractive in their diversity, and above all are more idyllic and poetical than the Engadine, which is more or less deficient in these qualities, and is even not free from a certain monotony in its rhythm,—if we may compare a district of Switzerland to a poetical composition.

But if, after the charm of novelty is past and curiosity has long been satisfied, the Engadine still continues to exercise its allurements and to attract men and women from the most distant lands, if the throng of its old admirers is annually reinforced by new comers, and if there are many persons who have for years past been regular summer visitors to this valley, then it must obviously be possessed of charms which, though differing in character from those of the Bernese Oberland and the much-frequented Lake of Lucerne, are at least quite as powerfully attractive.

The beauty of the Engadine does not lie on the surface, and is not of the dazzling kind; it lies deeper,—it must impress itself on the feelings, and then it becomes a matter of sympathy. And it is with a landscape as with the object of our affections,— sympathy of disposition is more than beauty, and unquestionably more enduring. The beauty of the Engadine consists above all in its primeval and undesecrated appearance, in its internal and external tranquillity, and in the harmony of all the features of the landscape.

One who has moved all his life in refined society, who has associated with his equals in station year after year in the drawing-room or the club according to the strict rules of etiquette, and who has been compelled to conform in everything to the prescribed formalities of fashion and the beau monde,— such a one would be surprised and agreeably impressed were he by chance to come in contact with unsophisticated children of nature, and, ascending as it were to the sources, become acquainted with the first rude beginnings of his dainty culture; a like effect is produced by a tour through the Engadine and a sojourn in its highland villages upon the inhabitants of cities and plains,—novel to them, at first, and strange, it is soon found to be refreshing, exhilarating, and animating.

Starting from Coire in the diligence near midnight, the traveller is carried past Churwalden, the Lonzer Haide, and Tiefenkasten, higher and higher, into an ever wilder and more desolate region, where vegetation dwindles until its only representatives are the modest but charming blossoms of the Alps. At length we reach the heights of the Julier Pass (7503 feet) with its two enigmatical columns—dedicated perchance of old to the sun-god Jul, a divinity fitly worshipped in this sublime temple of nature. And now, the road descending rapidly to Silvaplana, there emerge one after another from behind the larch forests the silvery summits of the mountains of the Engadine: Chapütschin, Piz Roseg, Corvatsch, Tremoggia, Piz Tschierva, Morteratsch, and the peerless Bernina, arrayed in spotless garments of snow and ice, and fringed at the base by a broad band of verdure.

Suddenly, gleaming like an emerald, a lake lies before us, and another, and another. A pleasant valley opens. The rapid Inn sparkles and glitters as it makes its way from one village to another. Substantially-built houses, churches, and hotels rise all around us, and above the entire scene spreads a deep-blue sky, so clear and fresh that it can be likened to no other but that of Southern Italy. The delightful air, redolent of newly-mown grass and of pine-woods—cool and refreshing though mild—breathes gently upon us; we draw a deep and joyous breath, — our mind is cognisant of a new delight !

There is nothing to confuse us here; the promised enjoyments are simple enough, no intricate maze of scenery
needs to be studied; but we recognise at once that the days
spent here will be full of variety.

As a valley landscape the Engadine is complete in itself.
The designation includes the main valley stretching from
north-west to south-east, together with numerous lateral
branches diverging from the main valley for the most part
at right angles, the whole lofty region extending in a wide
curve some sixty miles in length through the south-eastern
corner of Switzerland, and connecting Upper Italy with the
Tyrol and Southern Germany. The vast glacier-covered
moutain-ranges bounding the Engadine on the north and
south, and constituting independent groups, separate it on the
one side from the middle and north of Canton Grisons, with
which it is politically united—the extensive valleys of the Prättigau, Davos, Bergün, and Oberhalbstein—and on the other
side from the southern districts of Valtellina, Poschiavo,
Bormio, the Münsterthal, and Vintschgau.

The Engadine is traversed in its entire length by the
River Inn, which rises to the north of the Maloja Pass, at
the foot of the Longhino; its source being at a height of
about 6000 feet, the river has thus fallen nearly 2500 feet
by the time it reaches Martinsbruck.

These altitudes indicate that the Engadine is more
loftily situated than any other inhabited district of Europe,
with the exception perhaps of the valley of Avers, where
the village of Cresta is built at a height of more than 6000
feet above the level of the sea, and the Engadine is certainly
the only valley of anything like this altitude in which men
are found not leading an almost solitary life, seeking a
precarious subsistence as herdsmen and hunters, and occupying
mean and wretched huts, but assembled in well-regulated

communities, each numbering some hundreds of individuals, in comfortable, well-built, and indeed often wealthy and pretentious villages.

In regard to their manners and customs, mode of life, and language the people of the Engadine present several highly interesting features. They claim Roman descent, and the peculiarities of the race are more strongly marked here than in any other district of the Grisons. The general appearance of the inhabitants for the most part plainly indicates their Italian origin: dark hair, black, sparkling eyes, features usually interesting and often revealing a masculine type of beauty, a slender and yet powerful frame. They are chiefly engaged in pastoral and agricultural pursuits and in the rearing of cattle. Industries peculiar to the valley there are none; if the inhabitants are prosperous, their prosperity is due in part to the fine quality of the pasturage, but more especially to the profitable employment sought out for themselves by natives of the Engadine in foreign countries. For they are accustomed to emigrate to all parts of the world, and if in St. Petersburg or Paris, in Hamburg, Rome, or Naples a confectioner's shop or a café is found in a particularly flourishing condition and distinguished by its cleanliness from its surroundings, it will be safe to assume that the proprietor is from the Engadine. These voluntarily expatriated children of the mountains also engage in trade, and by steady industry combined with self-denial and thrifty habits—the latter perhaps being occasionally pushed somewhat too far – they realise competences. But whatever amount of wealth they may acquire, they still cherish the memory of their native valley, and return sooner or later from the busy town which has been the scene of their successful labours to the quiet village of their nativity; here they build for themselves an elegant house or pleasant villa, pass the evening of their days in ease and comfort, and leave to their children an honoured name and an assured livelihood.

This cosmopolitan character of the native of the Engadine accounts for his sociable and hospitable ways, his knowledge of the world, his freedom from restraint in intercourse with foreigners at home, his far-reaching experience, and his acquaintance with foreign languages. Almost all the male population speak three or more idioms with ease, and their German, being acquired in the schools, is the best heard anywhere in Switzerland.

But when they converse among themselves in their mother tongue, the natives of this valley are quite unintelligible even to visitors well versed in the principal languages of the continent. For this mountainous canton has a dialect of its own, known to philologists as Romansch or Rhæto-Romanic—from Rhætia, the ancient name of the province, which is still frequently spoken of by its inhabitants as "La Rezia" or "Aulta-Rezia".

"Rhæto-Romanic," says Lorenz Diefenbach, "claims attention as a sister tongue of Portuguese, Spanish, Provençal, Old French, Italian, and Roumanian. In all its tones we hear the rough, unadorned, and uncultured daughter of a beautiful mother, though indeed to the ear of the northerner, accustomed to much harsher sounds, it may seem comparatively soft. The stupendous character of the natural scenery is as it were reflected in the full-toned diphthongs as well as in the forcible and even hard pronunciation."

This language is still spoken by about 40,000 inhabitants of the Grisons, and in two main dialects,—Romansch and Ladin. Such a survival is really remarkable, for since the commencement of the modern era of free intercourse the existence of this ancient tongue has been threatened, and its

— 14 —

original purity greatly impaired, by two other languages,
namely Italian and the German patois spoken in Switzerland.
It is beyond doubt that this interesting language, Rhæto-
Romanic, is not an original or independent tongue, but merely
a subordinate member of the Romanic family of languages.
It appears to have been derived from a Latin dialect, probably
transplanted to these mountain solitudes by invasions of Roman
troops or by fugitives from Roman settlements. It is evident
that it retained its vitality, but it grew, like the Alpine vegetation, not so much in height as in breadth, while the other
dialects of the Latin underwent a constant process of development.

Nevertheless it possesses a tolerably extensive literature,
and of late years especially a number of worthy men have
exerted themselves in its behalf.

Among constant cherishers of their native tongue we
may mention the Planta family of Samaden, owners of large
estates both in the Upper and Lower Engadine, and the
families of Juvalta, Von Flugi-Aspermont, Von Sprecher, Ra-
scher, Von Travers, à Porta, etc.

A devoted labourer in the cause of preserving and cul-
tivating the Romansch dialect was Zaccaria Pallioppi of Celerina,
who contributed to its literature a number of fine poems. A
fellow-worker of his, Gian Frédric Caderas of Samaden, is
editor of the only newspaper printed in this language, the
"Fögl d'Engiadina," and has also published several volumes
of poetry, the last of which, entitled "Fluors Alpinas," (Alpine Flowers) contains, besides original pieces, numerous well-
executed translations from the German, in which the form
and metre of the original are carefully preserved. As a
specimen of these we reproduce Caderas's translation of the
"Lindenbaum," a song by Wilhelm Müller which is well known
through having been set to music by Schubert.

Il Tiglio.

("*Am Brunnen vor dem Thore, etc.*")

Al bügl davaunt la porta
As chatt'ün tiglio bel,
Sper el gugent tschantaiva,
Cur not regnaiv' in tschel.

Taglio aint in sa scorza
He pü d'ün nom zuond ober.
In led ed in leidezza
Stuvet tar el tschanter.

Allo darcho as drizza
Mieu pass cur tuot als-a-chür.
E l'ögl gugent s'eleva
Vers l'eter oler e pür.

Sa ramma dutsch suschurra
Am pera quasi dir:
"Ve, co, sper me reposa,
Tieu led giaro svanir!"

Il vent in vist 'am boffa
Crudo als mieu chape';
Nu'm mouv da mia plazza
E bain nun se perche!

Dalöntsch, dalöntsch sun uossa
Dal cher prüvo löet;
E vusch eau od chi clama:
"Lo pêsch tieu cour chattet!"

One of the "finest specimens of modern Rhætian literature, attractive and agreeable in its language, and thoroughly successful as a translation," is the version of the New Testament from the pen of Janet Menni, the venerable pastor of Samaden (Il Nuov Testamaint tradüt nel Dialect Romauntsch d'Engiadina). As a specimen we have selected a passage from the Gospel of St. Luke, chap. II., v. 8—12: "And there were in the same country shepherds abiding in the field."

"Ed in quella contredgia eiran pastuors sün la champagna ils quêls faivan guardia da not intuorn lur scossa. E mera, ün aungel del Segner als comparit, e la gloria del Segner splendurit intuorn els; ed els tmettan ficb. E l'aungel als dschct: Nun tmè! perche mera, eau's annunziesch üna granda algrezcha, chi vain ad arriver a tuot il pövel. Perche boz ais naschieu a vus il Salvedor, il quêl ais Cristo, il Segner, in la citted da David. E quaist as saja il signel: Vus chatteros ün infaunt fascho, miss in ün preseppen."

The Bible is not a forbidden book to the inhabitants of the Engadine; with the exception of the communes of Tarasp and Samnaun they belong to the Reformed Church. The epoch of the Reformation, moreover, marked a vast improvement in the condition of the people. The change was effected here in a singularly reasonable and patriarchal manner.

"It was in November of the year 1549," narrates Ernest Lechner, pastor of Stampa, "that an Italian who had crossed the Bernina Pass came to spend the night at a tavern then standing near the church of Pontresina. In the course of conversation the landlord, who was "ammann" or head man of the village, informed his guest that the parish was for the moment without a priest, and that he was expecting a meeting of the villagers in the tavern parlour that evening for the purpose of electing a fit person to the office. The visitor intimated that he was the reformer of the neighbouring valley of Poschiavo, Pietro Paolo Vergerio, formerly bishop of Capo d'Istria near Trieste. He expressed his willingness to address the assembly that evening, and the worthy landlord at once proceeded to ascertain the wishes of the villagers on this subject. At first many of them seemed unwilling to grant the Italian a hearing, but being curious to learn what manner of doctrines he taught they gave their consent. Vergerio delivered a fiery discourse in the tavern against the adoration of images, and his eloquence, though it disquieted many, was seconded to such good purpose by his commanding figure and venerable aspect, that he gained the applause of the majority of his audience, and was earnestly requested by them to preach in public before his departure. On the following day, therefore, which chanced to be a Sunday, he spoke from the pulpit on the subject of justification by faith. In front of the church the "ammann" inquired how the people liked the Italian. "So well," replied an aged man, "that he shall preach to us again to-morrow." The second sermon treated of the power of Christ's death. All the hearers were edified, and resolved forthwith to abolish the mass and to send for an evangelical preacher."

This Vergerio had fled to the Rhætian mountains to escape from the Roman inquisition; his brother, bishop of Pola, is said to have been poisoned. Vergerio established a printing-office in Poschiavo, became pastor of Vicosoprano, and won over in his simple manner eight parishes of the Grisons to the cause of the Reformation.

As in their acceptance of the new doctrines, so also in their political affairs the people usually exhibited calmness and moderation, never drawing the sword to maintain their rights as long as other means were open. But if their freedom or their honour was threatened, they knew how to assert themselves.

"The inhabitants of the Grisons are a people who from of old were famous for courage and manliness, and this reputation they have preserved down to the present day, in which they have shown a like intrepidity and heroism," says a writer of the sixteenth century, and in the old chronicles we find many a record of the impetuous bravery of this people, of their strength and firmness of purpose, and their love of independence combined with statesmanlike sagacity; they are credited with constant exertions in the cultivation of the mind, with virtue, hospitality, faith, piety, and reverence for all that men of worth hold sacred. Dwelling in their different valleys, these men felt themselves to be a single people, and in resistance to foreign usurpation and tyranny they ever united in a brotherhood dissoluble by death alone. Rhætia, no less than the Forest Cantons, has had her William Tell: Adam of Camogask was his name; and the heroic Benedict Fontana, who fell on the Malser Haide, was her Winkelried.

"It has justly been remarked," says Lechner, "that if an oppressed people would free itself, it should study the history of the Grisons. This history discloses a truly remarkable spectacle, a series of violent complications, bitter party dissensions, and treaties concluded for base and selfish ends; but great and noble deeds are also recorded."

As regards the point of honour the people of the Engadine were extremely sensitive. In the year 1543 Sebastian Münster, professor of Hebrew at the university of Basle, issued from the press of Henry Petri the "Universal Cosmography," a very rare work of 1400 folio pages embellished with woodcuts, maps, and diagrams. A copy of this book found its way into the Engadine, and the inhabitants were naturally curious to know what the author had to say about their home. To their chagrin they read that it "has many robbers" — *habet multos latrones.* This distasteful discovery was passed from mouth to mouth; both in the Upper and Lower Engadine the excitement it caused was intense, and if Basle had been a neighbouring canton war would certainly have been declared. Meeting after meeting was held, and the first result attained was that in all the copies on hand the calumnious passage was erased. But this did not satisfy the people of the Engadine. They sent a deputation to the senate of Basle with a demand that the author and the printer both be prosecuted for defamation.

The author had now been dead two years; the printer was still in the flesh, and was called upon to defend himself. He pleaded that he was not accustomed to read the works he published, that he left everything to his type-setters, and that among them was a native of the Engadine, a certain Stuppan, who had every interest to expunge the obnoxious passage. While characterizing Münster's description of the Engadine as slanderous, the senate acquitted the printer. But the deputation was not yet satisfied. It demanded and obtained a certificate from the senate stating that since the accusation against the Engadine was false and baseless, the inhabitants were not thereby insulted. Only now did the agitation cease.

The struggle for existence in this valley, where stones are more plentiful than bread, was of necessity a continuous and a severe one, and no doubt to the earliest settlers, accustomed to the warm and vivifying climate of Italy, the fight must have at first seemed hopeless. Their descendants, however, quickly learned to love the stony soil which had given them birth; but Nature, who in southern climes is so lavish in her gifts, was never a bountiful mother to the dwellers on these heights.

Oranges and lemons the traveller will scarcely expect to pluck here; but even the deciduous forest trees, which flourish so luxuriantly at a lower elevation, the beeches, oaks, elms, and maples, and the walnut and chestnut-trees such as fringe the Lake of Lucerne, are here quite absent. The walnut-tree is last seen far lower down, at Ried and Pfunds in the Tyrol, at a height of 3000 feet; cherry, pear, and apple-trees venture into the Lower Engadine, as far as Schuls (4700 feet); and even in Sils Maria, the highest village in the Upper Engadine, there stands a solitary cherry-tree, which ripens its fruit in

very warm years. In the gardens and on the window-sills
of the houses in Samaden, Pontresina, Celerina, St. Moritz,
and Sils, beautiful flowers may be seen, and spinach, cress
carrots, lettuce, &c., are also grown. Near Schuls and Ardetz
flourishing fields of rye are still met with, but this cereal
reaches its limit at Celerina. Summer barley, whose limit at
Davos and Bergün is several hundred feet lower down, ascends
in the Engadine, thanks to the favourable climate, as high as
Samaden and Campfèr.

Coniferous trees are predominant in the forests of the
Engadine, and next in importance come bushes of barberry
and wild rose. With the exception of here and there a few
stunted specimens of alders and birches, only coniferous trees
are to be found. But for these no slope is too steep, no ridge
too high; they thrive to perfection, and at 6500 feet the red
fir, at 7000 feet larches and pines (Pinus Cembra) find the
climate of the Engadine so well suited to them that they
reach a greater girth and altitude than elsewhere. Among the
larch-trees many specimens of really gigantic size may be
found.

The Pinus Cembra is the representative tree of the Engadine,
though unfortunately no longer to the same extent as formerly.
Before cultivation encroached upon its domain, this noble tree
spread over the entire canton, and formed the chief and
ubiquitous ornament of the highland regions; dense forests were
composed of it alone. At the present day it has been wofully
thinned out, and it is now mostly found interspersed among
other coniferous trees. Between Sils and Pontresina, however,
it still constitutes the main portion of the forests.

The flora, which is remarkable for the rarity of many of
the species and for vividness of colouring, attracts the attention
of every visitor to St. Moritz.

The fauna is also interesting, but limited space forbids us to enter into details; we can only refer the reader to Tschudi's magnificent work. Chief among the quadrupeds are the bear and the chamois, among birds the lammergeyer and the eagle; but the summer visitor is not likely to be favoured with a sight of any of these interesting creatures, whose numbers are carefully kept within due bounds by the skilful hunters of the Engadine.

Insects are represented here by numerous species, whose remarkable points are conditioned by the structural peculiarities of the flowers which afford them sustenance during their brief existence.

Among domestic animals the sheep plays an important rôle, and accompanying the flocks we meet the romantic figure of the Bergamask shepherd.

"It is a very ancient custom to drive the flocks of sheep up from the valleys of Brescia and Bergamo (where they pass the winter) to graze during the summer months on such pastures of the Grisons mountains as do not support their own herds of cattle. The respective communes derive a considerable revenue from this source, but it is by no means in proportion to the incalculable havoc which has been wrought during centuries past by these animals both upon the young trees and the pastures themselves; plants are torn up by the roots and the loose soil falls or is kicked down the steep slopes.

"Early in June numerous flocks of great, long-eared, half-starved animals make their appearance here; towards the end of August they are driven home again in fine condition, and then the long, coarse wool which they yield is disposed of to the large factories of Bergamo. Such migrations are interesting enough; the shepherds are accompanied by a certain number of cows and goats, and by asses laden with dairy utensils (and in autumn with dairy produce); large watch-dogs bring up the rear. The shepherds themselves, especially those hailing from the valleys of Seriana and Brembana in the province of Bergamo, are indeed remarkable objects, haughty in their bearing, with placid, furrowed, sun-burnt faces, unkempt beards, and long ringlets of black hair. Their head-dress is the peaked brown Calabrian hat, and over their shoulders a coarsely-made mantle of brown or white woollen stuff is thrown. They are a rough but honest race, reserved and taciturn in their demeanour, but for the most part handsome. They live on the mountains in the plainest and most frugal manner; a little polenta and cheese forms as a rule their only food, and the younger shepherds pass the night in the open air by the side of their flocks, often sheltered by some isolated rock. At times these shepherds pay a visit to the villages to purchase a supply of meal and salt ......

"Should the traveller chance to enter one of their châlets, he will find its rafters covered with the skins and dried flesh of sheep which have met with an untimely end by falling from some precipice, and he may well be dismayed by the smoke and dirt with which the hut reeks; nor is the odour emitted by the skins a remarkably agreeable one. The single apartment serves at once as kitchen, sleeping-room, and store-house; it is usually occupied by the oldest of the herdsmen, often men of advanced age."

As regards the dwellings in the villages of the valley, although they lack the snugness of the Bernese cottages, in which timber is so lavishly employed, they are on the whole well-built and neat, and are at any rate practical. Of course the dweller in the Engadine cannot build in the same style as the Italian, to whom a house is a matter of secondary importance; the climate of the valley is rigorous, and a house is absolutely necessary as a protection against the cold. Timber being scarce, stone is the material employed. The inhabitants are prosperous, and are therefore inclined to a certain degree of luxury. The style of architecture they favour is confined exclusively to this valley.

The doorway is wide and high, and must allow free passage to a well-loaded waggon. On entering we find ourselves in a spacious court with passages leading to the parlour and the kitchen; in the background are the stables, built on to the house. The rooms are low, in order that they may be more readily warmed, and are wainscotted as a further protection against the cold, which easily penetrates stone walls. The furniture and house utensils are of good quality, and the whole is kept scrupulously clean. For wainscotting the wood of *Pinus Cembra* was formerly exclusively used. This wood, being extremely resinous and of a strong but agreeable odour, harbours no insects; in time the resin comes to the surface and covers it with a kind of varnish, but will not bear paint of any kind.

The windows of the Engadine houses are remarkable; they are small and narrow, widening towards the exterior to admit as much light as possible. In houses of recent construction this old plan has been abandoned, no doubt at the expense of the temperature of the rooms, which in the older houses is often brought to an unbearable degree by means of the huge porcelain stoves and the various contrivances for retaining the heat.

The exterior of these dwellings presents, as already intimated, a certain air of comfort, security, and hospitality, and they are always kept neat and trim in appearance, while the wood and ironwork are made as ornamental as possible, the latter being frequently gilded. The gardens surrounding the houses, and the flowers in front of the windows, conduce in no small degree to the attractive appearance of these dwellings. It is indeed marvellous to see how splendidly such plants as violets, wallflowers, tulips, verbenas, ranunculuses, pelargoniums, fuchsias, anemones, phloxes, convolvuluses, flags, blue-bells, and poppies thrive at this great elevation.

No one that wanders through the Engadine can fail to be favourably impressed with what he sees; and this impression is confirmed and strengthened on our becoming more closely acquainted with the valley and its inhabitants as seen in a smaller circle. We shall now describe such a circle, and henceforth concentrate our attention upon that part in which the health-resort of St. Moritz is situated, namely the Upper Engadine.

THE UPPER ENGADINE.

"Light is the breath we draw in this pure air,
Then haste, O wanderer, the boon to share;
Flower and fountain, peak and field
New stores of health and vigour yield!"

THE etymology of the name "Engadine" is most probably connected with the geographical position of the *Upper* Engadine. It is generally thought to be derived from "en co d'Oen," equivalent to "in capite Oeni," — "at the head or source of the Inn," and the Upper Engadine lies, as is well known, near the sources of that river.

Other explanations have been put forth. For instance, in a document of the tenth century the valley is designated "Vallis Eniatina," in the Celtic form "Endjathina" (from *enjath*, water-land) and if this derivation be accepted, the name Engadine would accordingly signify a district along a river.

But in the oldest Rhæto-Romanic writings the name, according to Rausch, is spelled Oengadina, where not the last syllable, as in the first etymology, but the first syllable *En, In, Oen (Oenus,* Inn) would refer to the river, while *gadina* or *giadina* must be taken as the diminutive of the Teutonic tribe of *Gad*, supposed to have entered the Engadine at the time of the Migration of Peoples; but the primary meaning of *gad* was "an elongated, narrow space," a lane (German *gasse*) and this would seem applicable enough to our valley.

Modern etymologists have dispossessed the ancient divinities of many a hill and dale, and destroyed the romance attached to them by tradition. Let us then stick to the first explanation, if we must have one (for perhaps all are erroneous) and also rest satisfied with the derivation of the name of the capital of the Engadine, Samaden, from *Summnum Oeni*, in Romansch *Sommo d'Oen.*

But as for the suggested interpretation of the name Engadine as *Acqua Deng*, from the farmhouse of Deng or Degn in the vicinity of the inn on the Maloja Pass, we can safely decline to accept it.

For us therefore the beautiful Engadine remains the beautiful "valley of the Inn."

The valley is divided, as already mentioned, into two unequal parts, namely the Upper Engadine, about 24 miles, and the Lower Engadine, some 33 miles in length. This division is political (the Upper Engadine with its 11 communes is included in the district of Maloja, while the 12 communes of the Lower Engadine constitute an independent district), but it coincides with the natural topographical divisions.

The character of the scenery in the upper and lower sections of the valley is quite distinct, the Upper Engadine showing to the greater advantage in this respect. Here the mountain-ranges bounding the valley are from one and a half to three miles apart; ample room being thus afforded for human habitations and settlements, a high state of cultivation has been reached. Between the mountains, on either bank of the river, lies an expanse of fertile meadow land, fringed at the base of the mountains with a narrow zone of forest, in the rear of which the spacious Alpine pastures extend up to the precipitous rocky escarpment forming the summit of the ridge, which is everywhere of nearly uniform height. From above

Campfér, near the Baths of St. Moritz, and Piz La Margna.

this ridge a long array of snowy peaks look down upon the smiling valley.

The Upper Engadine extends as far as Punt-auta or Pontalta, leading below Scanfs to the deep gorge between Cinuschel and Brail, where in the ancient epoch of chronic warfare a kind of Chinese wall five hundred paces in length was carried transversely across the valley and completed the separation between the Upper and Lower Engadine. The Lower Engadine extends from this point to the Pomartin (Punt-Martin), in German *Martinsbruck*. Here the mountain-ridges approach closer together; the valley widens and contracts alternately, the Inn traversing it most of the distance in a ravine so deep and narrow that the river is hidden from sight. But little space is left for human dwellings, so that the villages are perforce perched on the lofty terraces of the mountain-sides; the terraces of the northern chain being more spacious, convenient, and sunny, they are therefore more populous. These villages, the chief of which are Zernetz and Schuls— Zuort and Scharl are mere assemblages of huts—lack the trim and comfortable appearance which characterizes the villages of the Upper Engadine.

Just as the entire Engadine is divided into two main portions, so also the Upper Engadine is again separated into two plainly-marked halves by a rocky ledge running straight across the valley. On this ledge stands St. Moritz, the most important place, though not the political capital; the latter distinction is claimed by Samaden.

Below this ledge or shelf, in the north-eastern half of the valley, lie the villages of Bevers, Campovasto or Camogask, Ponte, where the high-road descends from the Albula Pass, Madulein, with the ruins of the famous castle of Guardavall, Zuz, and Scanfs.

In the upper half, above Samaden, we find Celerina, St. Moritz, Campfèr, Silvaplana, and the two Sils; from the latter the summit of the Maloja or Maloggia Pass is soon reached.

This Pass is the most elevated point in the valley of the Inn, being about 5600 feet above the sea-level. It divides the valley of Bergell, known in Roman times as Prægallia, from the upper valley of the Inn. We are here standing on the water-parting of two seas, the Black Sea and the Adriatic; or we may even say of three, for from the Septimer a torrent descends to the Rhine and ultimately finds its way to the North Sea.

But let us descend again to our valley. Leopold von Buch has given an excellent description of the Upper Engadine, which he entered by crossing the Bernina Pass.

"On reaching the valley it seems almost as though we had not yet left the Bernina behind, and it would scarcely surprise us to find ourselves again among châlets and Alpine huts. But to see such a valley—which in any other situation would itself be a lofty mountain, and the ascent to which has occupied several days—swarming with inhabitants and occupied in its entire extent by large and well-built villages, cannot fail to excite the astonishment of the traveller. The limit at which trees will grow is but a little above the bottom of the valley, the meadows are gay with Alpine flowers, and snowy summits rise on either side in immediate proximity to the rich pastures. But the inhabitants do not occupy Alpine huts; often their dwellings might rather be taken for palaces, so spacious, imposing, and elegant are they. Balconies with finely-wrought iron railings, broad flights of steps, symmetrically-divided windows breaking the monotony of the white surface of the walls,—neither these nor the numerous carriages rolling along the excellently-kept highway, point to Alpine herdsmen as the inhabitants of the valley. Such a spectacle is scarcely to be found elsewhere in Europe, and in view of this activity and cultivation we would gladly regard as an illusion the abrupt cessation of all life on the mountain-ridges hard by. But it is no illusion."

Every valley presupposes mountains, and we will here insert a few brief notes regarding those of the Upper Engadine.

They belong to the main southern chain of the Swiss Alps, of which they constitute, under the name of the Grisons Alps, one of the principal divisions. They may in turn be subdivided into a western range, extending from the Lukmanier to the Splügen, with the Rheinwaldhorn as culminating-point; a middle chain, dominated by the Piz d'Err; a northern range, comprising the Albula Alps, the Selvretta Alps, the group of the Jamthaler Ferner, the highest peak of which is Piz Kesch; and the South Grisons or Engadine Alps, also called, after their loftiest summit (12,294 feet), the Bernina group.

The Bernina group is a so-called "central mass," that is to say, both in respect to the period of its formation and to its geological structure it may be properly treated as an independent whole.

The "central mass" of the Bernina may again be divided into seven members, four of which, namely the Bernina proper, the Languard mountains, the mountains of Piz Ot and the south side of the Albula, and the Julier mountains call for notice in a description of the Upper Engadine.

The Bernina mountains, which embrace the loftiest summits of the Upper Engadine, are bounded on the north and east by the Engadine lakes, the Languard-Alp, the upper Bernina Pass, and the Lake of Poschiavo, on the south and west by the Val Malenco and the Mureto Pass. The most important peaks are Piz Bernina, Piz Roseg, Piz Zupo, Piz Palü,

Tschierva, Morteratsch, Cresta Agiuza, Pers, Albris, Rosatsch, and Surlei, consisting almost entirely of plutonic rocks (granite, syenite, &c.); while the Chapütschin, Sella, Cambrena, Carral, Verona, Corvatsch, and Margna are composed of crystalline schists, Tremoggia and Alv of limestone, and the Moro and others of green slate.

On the lofty plateau of the Bernina Pass, at an altitude of 7283 feet, lie four little lakes, called respectively the Blaue See, Lago Nero, Lago Bianco, and Lago della Scala. Among the streams of this district we may mention the Morteratsch-Bach, springing from the glacier of the same name, the Flatz-Bach, which forms a magnificent cascade a short distance from the glacier from which it flows, and the Languard-Bach, the falls of which are visible from the Pontresina road.

Between the Flatz-Bach and the Inn, in the vicinity of the Lake of St. Moritz, the pretty little Lake of Statz is situated; and here too rise the syenite walls of Piz Rosatsch, "whose interior forms the secret laboratory for the mineralisation of the medicinal springs."

The bottom of the valley consists principally of crystalline schists, and in the trough-like hollows of these rocks four beautiful sheets of water have been formed: the Lakes of St. Moritz, Campfèr, Silvaplana, and Sils.

The Languard mountains are the second "central mass" of the Upper Engadine, and may be regarded as the north-eastern prolongation of the Bernina, although their predominant components are crystalline schists. On the north-west they are bounded by the valley of Campovasto, opposite the embouchure of the Albula Pass, as far as St. Moritz. In the south-west and south their limits are defined by the limestone ridges on the Lake of Statz, Val Languard, Pischa, the upper Val del Fain, and the Pass of La Stretta, leading into the Val di Livigno, in the south-east by the Val del Fain. On the north and north-east the Languard group borders on the limestone mountains beginning at the outlet of Val Campovasto and extending to the Spöl, near Zernetz.

The geological centre of this group is not Piz Languard (10,715 feet), but the glacier-covered Piz Vadret (10,403 feet). Other summits are Piz Prunas (10,347 feet) and Piz Prunella (9816 feet), enclosing the three valleys of Val Prunas, Val Prunella, and Plaun de Vachas, which afterwards unite in the Val Chamuera, and open at right angles into the valley of the Inn near Campovasto. Above the Val Chamuera are the smaller valleys of Champagna, Murailg, and Müsellas. Between the two former lie the heights of Muottas (7992 feet), much frequented by excursionists.

The Piz Ot and Albula mountains, the third "central mass" of the Upper Engadine, form the opposite wall of the valley, between Ponte and St. Moritz. This group is bounded in the north by the Albula Pass, in the west by the Suvretta Pass, in the east by the valley of the Inn, and in the south by the limestone mountains of St. Moritz.

The central point of the range is Piz Ot (10,659 feet), and not far from it, above Samaden, stands Piz Padella (9458 feet).

Here opens the Val Celerina, the left side of which is formed by Piz Padella, the right by Piz Nair (10,039 feet). A continuation of this valley, known as the Val Saluver, terminates in a pass leading to the Lago di Suvretta, above which towers Piz Suvretta (10,085 feet). From this mountain one can descend into the Bevers-Thal, which extends in a crescent shape around Piz Ot and opens into the valley of the Inn at Bevers.

The fourth and last "central mass" is formed by the granite mountains of the Julier, commencing at Piz Munteratsch and extending in a south-westerly direction as far as

---

the Septimer Pass. Its boundaries are: on the north-east Piz Nair and the mountains of St. Moritz, towards the south-east the valley of the Upper Engadine. On the right side of the Val Suvretta stands Piz Munteratsch (11,105 feet) and Piz Albana (10,170 feet), both sloping off on the south towards the Julier Pass (7503 feet), while opposite them on the other side of the pass rise Piz Püluschin (9898 feet) and Piz Lagref (9721 feet). Here granite is the only rock; gneiss and mica-slate reappear lower down, below the road.

With the mountains extending across to the Septimer, Piz da Graves (10,400 feet), Piz Nalar, and Piz Longhino (9120 feet), we have arrived at the uppermost point of the Upper Engadine considered as the valley of the Inn. Here lies the Lake of Longhino, mentioned above. It is chiefly remarkable from a geographical point of view: its waters find their way into three different seas.

In respect to climate, vegetation, and the life led by its inhabitants, this lofty region may be compared to many lands in northern latitudes; it has even been called the "Siberia of the Alps." Various proverbs are current regarding its climate. One of them says that in the Upper Engadine they have "nine months of winter and three months of cold weather." An Italian rhyme runs: "Engiadina, terra fina, se non fosse la pruina," "the Engadine were fine, I ween, if the hoar frost had not been." But why heed the witticisms of the delicate children of the South, whose own genial climate renders them impatient of the bracing air of the Alps?

In the summer months the sun burns fiercely enough in the Engadine, and the grass in the meadows and on the mountain-slopes is often parched and withered. But still the heat bears no comparison to that of southern lands. The air of the Engadine is always pleasant, refreshing, and salubrious. One's spirits cannot fail to be cheered by the light and exhilarat-

ing atmosphere, the cloudless azure sky, the lovely flowers
adorning the meadows, the fresh and dewy verdure of the
Alpine pastures. Summer is nowhere more enjoyable than here,
and it is in summer that the Engadine is chiefly visited, in
accordance with the advice tendered in a Romansch proverb:

> Chi l'Engiadina voul vair bella,
> Vegn' üna vouta l'ann,
> E que intuorn San Gian.

"Let him who would see the Engadine in its beauty come
once a year, and that about St. John's day."

A still better season would be the spring-time of this upland valley, the beginning of July. April and May are winter
months here. Precisely in April and May the Engadine is at
its worst; the melting snow is pouring down the slopes in
muddy torrents, and the roads and paths are in anything but
a pleasant condition. But in July the sun commences his work
in earnest: everywhere he calls forth the verdure, regardless
of the snowfields so near at hand; leaf-buds and flower-buds
unfold in rapid succession, until the entire land becomes one
garden. The grass in the meadows soon stands as high as corn,
and when towards the end of July hay-making begins, the
peasants have a merry time of it. The joy is indeed somewhat
brief, for towards the end of August the nights become cold
again, and the hoar frost, the *pruina* of the Italians, falls. But
this is the time for tourists and mountaineers to visit the
Engadine; the snow has quite disappeared, and the glaciers
have retreated farther back. The air is calm and still, and so
clear that far distant objects appear to have advanced many
miles nearer; the prospect enjoyed from the mountain-summits
is therefore very extensive. The weather is at this time settled
in character, and often remains cool and clear until October.
True it is that the valley is no longer clad in the emerald-
green dress of early summer; the meadows have already

assumed a ruddy tint; but now the autumnal hues of the forests delight the eye, — the yellow foliage of the larches interspersed among the dark pines.

Winter in the Engadine has its amenities too. Far from standing in dread of it, the inhabitants are enthusiastic in its praise, and the number of winter visitors is constantly on the increase. Storms of wind, and snow, and ice are of course not wanting at this altitude, but a spell of foul weather is invariably succeeded by a series of clear, dry days when the sun shines brightly and the sky is of as deep a blue as in spring-time. There are new effects of light to be admired now: the glitter of the sunbeams upon the snow-crowned mountains and acclivities, sunset in this world of icy summits, a moon-light night, a starry sky—all are so full of charm, so sublime, and so novel that enthusiasm for this beautiful and quiet season is easily understood.

And then what enjoyments has this winter to offer! The surface of the frozen snow soon forms magnificent roads over which glide the sledges with their tinkling bells. Only the inhabitants of the Engadine know what such a "*schlitteda*" means:

"Il tschel ais pür. D'ün alv linzöl vestida
Bellissm' al sguard appera nossa val;
Ad ir in schlitta l'ora bell' invida......
O profittò, mieus chers, del carneval!"
(*Caderas*).

And in the gaieties of these "schlittedas," the merry-makings of the Carnival, the balls and other social amusements of this light-hearted little people, numerous visitors, attracted by the perfect purity of the atmosphere, have now begun to take part.

It is a people sound in mind and body, for the climate is indeed a healthy one. Cold is seldom prejudicial to health when accompanied by a dry atmosphere; it is only rapid variations in the degree of moisture that are injurious, and accordingly the unhealthiest time is when the snows are melting.

Chronic and constitutional diseases are rare, and tend to gradually disappear in families that have immigrated from other quarters. Among infants the chief mortality takes place during the winter; it may indeed be said that in the Engadine the first two years of life are attended with the most peril; if they are passed in safety a great age is usually reached, and with comparative immunity from sickness.

After an experience extending over many years, Dr. A. Biermann has given a resumé of the frequency with which certain diseases occur. Rickets and scrofula are extremely rare; caseous infiltration and tuberculosis are also among the least common maladies. Anæmia and chlorosis occur occassionally among persons in unfavourable circumstances of life. In winter infants are liable to attacks of croup, which proves their most fatal enemy. Epidemic diseases, such as measles, scarlet fever, small-pox, and hooping-cough also occur here at times, diphtheria and typhoid fever very seldom; cholera is unknown; imported malarial fever soon dies out. Owing to the character of the climate, diseases usually take an acute form, and chronic maladies are therefore almost absent. Chronic bronchitis and emphysema are rarely met with. On the other hand inflammatory diseases with an acute course are endemic here, — especially, as already mentioned, at the time of the melting snows; among them we may specify affections of the respiratory organs, rheumatism, with its sequelæ, heart disease, neuralgias, gastric and intestinal catarrh resulting from exposure and from dietetic causes, and, somewhat frequently, catarrh of the conjunctiva.

We are naturally interested in the vital statistics of the place in which we live or to which we resort to be cured of our maladies. Dr. Biermann gives the following table:

Table of Mortality in the Upper Engadine (Pop. 3583) during the years 1871, 1872, and 1873. Total number of deaths 189.

	Sils	Silvaplana	St. Moritz	Celerina	Samaden	Pontresina	Ponte-Campovasto	Zuz	Scanfs
In childbed (mothers or children)	4	2	2	—	5	4	1	1	—
Old age	3	2	3	2	5	3	5	6	1
Apoplexy	2	1	—	1	1	3	1	1	3
Inflammation of the brain and its processes	--	1	1	—	2	—	—	—	5
Heart disease	1	1	-	2	1	—	-	1	
Rheumatism and gout	—	6	1	1	1	—	--	2	2
Inflammation of the respiratory organs and their processes	5	1	6	—	2	3	—	1	—
Phthisis	—	—	--	1	--	1	1	2	1
Acute and chronic diseases of the abdominal organs	3	4	4	5	8	2	—	6	4
Diseases of the kidneys, bladder, and generative organs	—	1	1	-	—	—	1	1	3
Typhoid fever	1	1	-	—	2	1	—	1	1
Diphtheria	—	...	—	-	9	—	-	—	—
Acute exanthemata	--	-	—	—	—	1	1	—	—
Nervous diseases		1	---	-	—	—	1	2	—
Cancer	-	1	—	—	—	2	—	—	1
Surgical diseases and accidents	1	—	2	—	2	—	—	—	1
	19	22	21	10	39	21	11	23	23

N.B. The deaths which occurred during these three years among visitors are not included. As regards deaths from phthisis it is not in each case recorded whether and for how long the victim had resided in other districts.

Having already given a brief sketch of the climate of the
Upper Engadine about as it would impress a tourist, who
usually distinguishes only between "fine" and "wet" weather,
it remains to give a somewhat more scientifically exact description of the climate. Dr. C. Brügger devoted considerable
time to the matter, and published the result of his researches
in a climatological work containing among other things several
tables of averages; Dr. August Husemann gives us these
observations together with his own and those of Major P.
Candrian (stationed during the summer months in the Kurhaus
at St. Moritz).

In the first place the vegetation of the Upper Engadine
is compared with that of other mountain districts, to the
advantage of the Engadine; for while in the Harz timber-
trees reach their limit at a height of 3526 feet, in the Riesen-
gebirge at 4691 feet, in the northern limestone mountains of
Switzerland, the Tyrol, and Bavaria at from 5800 to 6400
feet, entire forests of well-developed specimens of pine, larch,
and fir are met with in the Upper Engadine at an elevation
of 7465 feet above the sea-level, and on the north side of
the mountains. Neither in the Caucasus nor in the Pyrenees
do forest trees attain so high a limit. We have already
enumerated some of the useful and ornamental plants found
flourishing in the gardens of the loftiest villages.

A comparison of the limit of perpetual congelation in the
Engadine and in other districts of the Alps is also favourable
to the former. In the Upper Engadine the snow-line is nowhere
below 10,072 feet, while in Bavaria it is 2525 feet lower, in
the rest of Switzerland 1340 feet, and in the Pyrenees 1115
feet lower. The well-known Grindelwald Glacier in the Bernese
Oberland descends to within 3350 feet of the sea-level, whereas
the Bernina Glacier descends even on the north side no lower
than to about 6500 feet.

In regard to the annual fall of snow, too, the Engadine shows favourable statistics. It is true that snow lies on the ground to a depth of from one and a half to four and a half feet during almost half the year, and long-continued observations have given for the average duration of the winter snows a period of 173 days; but were not the conditions in the Engadine exceptionally favourable, the average would be much higher, for in the Eastern Alps, at a like elevation, snow lies on the ground 196 days.

The visitor may even chance to meet with a snowstorm in the middle of the summer season, but this is not to be wondered at, for in the Bavarian Alps snow often falls in summer at a height of less than 5250 feet. In the Upper Engadine, however, this summer snow rarely falls on the bottom of the valley, but is confined to the forest-covered slopes, and even then it is almost invariably the precursor of fine clear weather.

We may therefore safely say that no mountainous region in Europe is able to boast such favourable climatic conditions as the Upper Engadine at a like elevation; in this respect St. Moritz is unique, enjoying as it does as mild a climate as places situated from one to two thousand feet lower.

Those who are interested, from the point of view either of the meteorologist or of the physician in the minuter variations of climate at St. Moritz will do well to study the following tables.

Mean Temperatures of the Summer Months and of the Season during the ten years 1856—1865, according to Prof. C. Brügger.

(In degrees Fahrenheit).

Month	5 a.m.	1 p.m.	9 p.m.	Mean daily temperature	Daily fluctuation of temperature
June...	41.57	57.27	44.74	49.55	15.69
July...	43.55	61.28	49.85	52.46	49.67
August	42.98	60.62	48.70	51.67	49.64
September	38.64	54.23	43.16	45.60	47.48
Season (21 June to 20 Sept. ...	42.31	59.43	44.07	50.63	49.01

Mean Temperatures of the Summer Months and of the Season during the seven years 1867—1873.
(Dr. Husemann, from Caudrian's daily observations).
(In degrees Fahrenheit).

Month	7 a.m.	1 p.m.	9 p.m.	Mean daily temperature	Daily fluctuation of temperature
June...	45.95	55.61	44.74	48.74	43.89
July...	50.79	62.48	47.87	54.57	45.39
August	46.92	59.50	48.11	51.51	45.86
September	40.58	54.96	44.00	46.45	47.83
Season (21 June to 20 Sept. ...	47.31	59.77	48.30	51.80	45.89

Average of the Weather Conditions for the Summer Months
and the Season during the Fourteen Years 1860—1873.
(Dr. Husemann, from Candrian's Observations).

Month	Cloudless on days	Cloudy on days	Fog on days	Rain on days	Snow on days	Thunder on days
June	17.9	12.1	1.4	7.2	0.93	1.4
July	21.9	9.1	3.3	7.5	0.07	3.7
August	21.5	9.5	3.3	7.4	0.36	2.2
September	21.4	8.6	5.4	6.1	1.86	0.8
Season (21 June to 20 Sept.) ...	63.9	28.1	10.8	21.4	1.57	7.6

A comparison of the weather at St. Moritz, as shown in
the last table, with that of other Alpine health-resorts will
show that nowhere else is the number of cloudy days so small
in proportion to the number of clear days. During the three
months embraced in the "season" the average is only 28 cloudy
and 31 rainy days against 64 clear days. For each rainy day
there are thus three days of sunshine. This is a point of great
importance. Compare for instance with this the climatic health-
resort of Pisa, under an Italian sky: here there are on an
average 122 rainy days in each year, or in other words every
third day is a rainy one! A notable difference this!

The full meaning of a clear and sunshiny summer day in
a sheltered Alpine valley at an altitude of 6000 feet above
the sea, where all the life and development of organised
nature is compressed into the short span of a few summer
months with an energy which produces a truly intoxicating
effect upon a sensitive temperament, is known only to those
who have experienced it and freely surrendered themselves to
its enchantments.

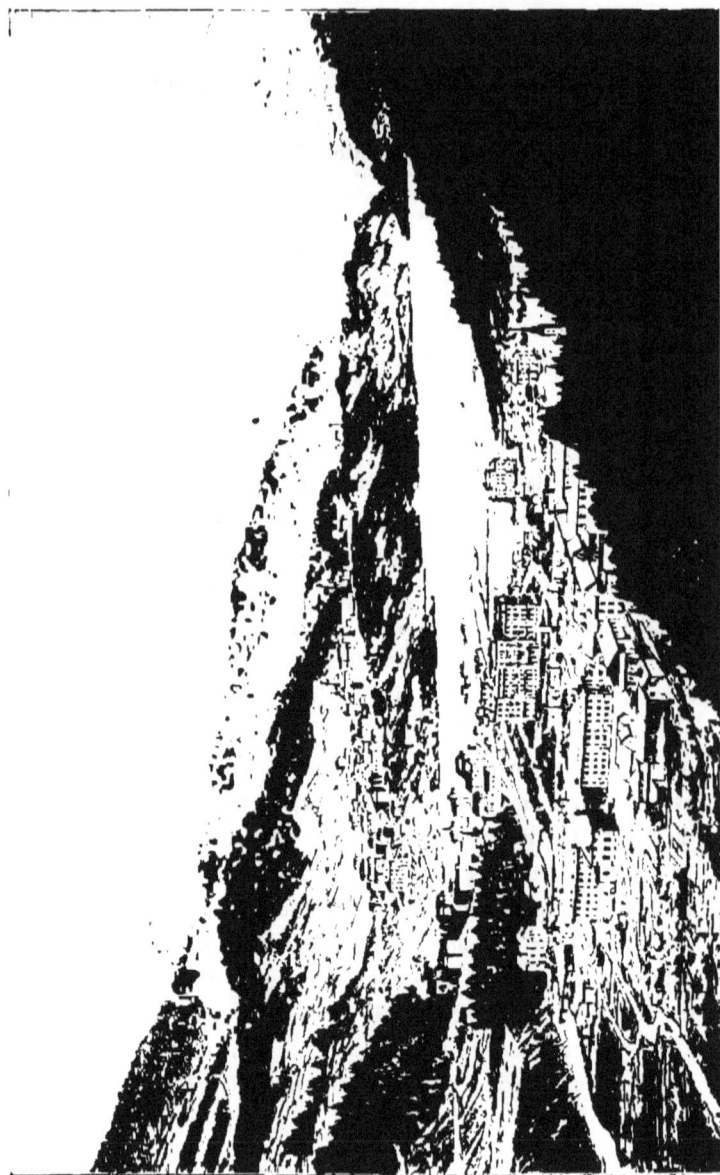

THE BATHS OF ST. MORITZ.

"Here by this little well sit down and rest,
To thee as unto me it shall be blest,
It is a fountain precious, mild, and pure,
Potent the ills of suffering man to cure."

MEDICINAL springs flow in every canton of Switzerland,
but none of them possess such an abundance of effi-
cacious mineral waters as the canton of Grisons, which deserves
all its fame in this respect; scarcely a valley, however small
and sequestered, is without one. It is easy to recall a long
list of celebrated wells, known to the inhabitants since the
earliest times, and now familiar to the ear of every physician;
for instance St. Bernhardin, the Passug-Quelle in the Val
Rabiosa, the St. Peters-Quelle near Tiefenkasten, the Donatus-
Quelle at Solis, the Baths of Alveneu in the Albula-Thal, Le
Prese in the Valle Poschiavo, the celebrated springs of *Tarasp-
Schuls* in the Lower Engadine, and Serneus.

But in this respect again the Upper Engadine has been
the most richly dowered, for the queen of all spas, and one
which has enjoyed its reputation during centuries, is St. Moritz
with its chalybeate springs.

This spa deserves the crown, and indeed its name is known
and its claims are recognised throughout the civilised world.

Nor is it too much to say that the Engadine as a whole,
and the Upper Engadine in particular, primarily owes its fame
and reputation not to its lofty mountains, not to its vast glaciers,
not to its swift-flowing river, but exclusively to its chalybeate

springs—the little springs flowing in silence and secresy at
St. Moritz. But of late years its reputation has increased in a
very important degree (we may as well call special attention
to this fact at the outset) for the reason that not only the
medicinal springs, but the climatic advantages and effects of
the valley are beginning to be valued as they deserve.

The peerless Alpine climate of the Upper Engadine has a
remarkably tonic and invigorating effect upon the system, and
its influence makes itself felt in a like manner with that of
the internal and external use of the chalybeate springs, namely
by *promoting the formation of blood* and *strengthening the
entire system*, so that these two factors—the bracing Alpine
climate and the chalybeate springs — mutually supplement and
confirm the effects produced by each. It is owing to the fortu-
nate combination of these two factors that brilliant results
have been attained at St. Moritz even in desperate cases, in
which the most famous chalybeate springs of the lowlands would
have availed little.

Although the excellent effect of the mountain climate of
the Upper Engadine is constantly becoming more widely known,
and several of the more favourably situated villages have already
begun to be used to a considerable extent as *winter health-
resorts*, it is right to state here in express terms that owing
to the position of the *Baths of St. Moritz* they would not be
well suited for the reception of winter visitors, and they are
for this reason *exclusively* devoted to the purposes of a summer
climatic health-resort and watering-place.

We will therefore turn our attention in the first place to
the springs, and to the arrangements which their native guar-
dians have made for the benefit of the visitors who flock hither
from all parts of the world.

All who are acquainted with the Baths must agree in
giving them this testimony: *St. Moritz is a high-class watering-*

*place, supplied with every modern convenience, and fully able
to meet every requirement of those who visit it.*

An impartial and thoroughly competent witness, the well-
known traveller Fritz Wernick, writes thus concerning the
exterior aspect of these "interesting international baths": "It
is difficult to conceive a more perfect contrast than that afforded
by the hour's walk which brings us from the unpretentious
village of Pontresina to this watering-place. Leading across
foaming glacier-torrents, past wooded heights and miniature
lakes, it is a pleasant and interesting stroll. But from the brow
of the last hilly ridge, on which stands a farm-house, a pleasure-
resort of the two neighbouring villages, we look down into
quite another world. Over the Lake of St. Moritz glide boats
and gondolas manned by Italian gondoliers. Immense palace-
fronts rise from the verdant surface of the ground. The Baths
have long since made themselves independent of the old mother-
colony, the village. Half-a-dozen extensive four-storied hotels,
a Kurhaus, and by its side the spa building and bathing establishment constitute the place which designates itself the Baths
of St. Moritz (St. Moritz-Bad). But these edifices are no longer
sufficient for the numerous guests. The season here lasts scarcely
more than two months, July and August, and all who come
hither in search of health come at this time. Ladies suffering
from anæmia seem to be specially benefited by the water, but
every shattered or debilitated system, every frame growing weak
and withered from the approach of old age lauds the rejuve-
nating power of the waters of St. Moritz—this true fountain
of youth. Adelaide Ristori, who for years past has made proof
of their effect, is by no means the only regular frequenter of
the baths. Crowned heads and princely families, statesmen and
diplomatists—Frenchmen and Italians for the most part, but
also Americans, Englishmen, and Germans—return year by
year to these health-giving waters. No doubt their mineral

constituents are extremely powerful, but it is certain that they
would not work such wonders if they issued from the ground
at a lower level."
Nowhere has the hotel question been so well and so
satisfactorily settled as at St. Moritz. The above-mentioned
"half dozen" hotels meet all the varied requirements in respect
to situation and arrangement, and the "Six" are to-day in a
position to quarter and provide for a small army. Their names are:

1. Kurhaus St. Moritz.	4. Hof St. Moritz.
2. Hôtel Victoria.	5. Hornbacher's Hôtel Engadinerhof.
3. Hôtel du Lac.	6. Hôtel Bellevue.

The Kurhaus contains 300 beds, Hôtel Victoria 250, Hôtel
du Lac 250, Hof St. Moritz 50, Hornbacher's Hôtel Engadinerhof 50, Hôtel Bellevue 100—a thousand visitors therefore find
here "where to lay their head," and although this number
would make up the "small army" mentioned above, it is very
desirable that early application be made to the managers of
the hotels—if possible in spring—for, owing to their proximity
to the springs, the concourse of visitors in the *hotels of
St. Moritz-Bad* is very great.

The *Kurhaus* is the oldest building,—at least that portion
of it comprising the two wings which lie in the same line of
frontage as the springs and baths; adjoining this at a right
angle is the beautiful and elegant modern building, with façades
looking east and west, while a middle wing contains the
magnificent dining-hall. All the rooms, both of the old and
new building, are connected by covered passages with the baths
and the Trinkhalle, and as regards other conveniences also the
Kurhaus is in itself an epitome of a small but comfortable
town. The visitor finds a physician in the house, pleasant conversation and ladies' saloons, a concert hall, restaurants, 18
private drawing-rooms with balconies, 219 sleeping apartments

with the above-stated number of beds, a Catholic chapel, French
chapel, post and telegraph office, banker's office, bazaars,
hair-dresser's, a band of Milanese musicians (engaged in common with the Hôtels du Lac and Victoria), stables, coach-
houses for private carriages; bathing cabinets, douches, milk-
cure room; for excursions in the environs carriages, saddle-
horses, guides, and porters can always be had. The movements
of this immense apparatus are directed and controlled in an
admirable manner; it is perfectly noiseless in its operation.
The same may be said of all the hotels in St. Moritz, and
this is an advantage which should not be undervalued; the
benefit to one's nerves is far from insignificant.

The kitchen is excellent, and only very seldom has it
been known to incur the censure of the most fastidious; even
then a valid excuse is found in the great difficulty of procuring
provisions with regularity in this remote Alpine valley.

What we have said in praise of the Kurhaus may justly
be said also of the other hotels, which without exception make
it their object to satisfy the requirements of all their guests
from the highest to the lowest.

The *Hôtel Victoria* is also a noble building, and whoever
knows the Hôtel Bernina at Samaden, and is aware that the
same Fanconi is also proprietor of the Hôtel Victoria at St.
Moritz, expects great things from this house, and will not
find himself disappointed. For the Hôtel Victoria is also a first-class
establishment, with 20 fine saloons and 159 bed-rooms, meeting
every modern requirement in respect to comfort and sanitation.
It is built opposite the new wing of the Kurhaus, standing
transversely across the valley, its principal façade facing the
south; its side fronts face the east and west, and we may
regard it as the fourth side of the Kurplatz in the neighbourhood
of the Trinkhalle, the third being formed by the Villa Inn
(on the left bank of the river), an appendage of the Kurhaus.

The equally high-class *Hôtel du Lac* also occupies a
magnificent position close to the bridge over the river and to
the baths. Its elegant façade faces full south, and the windows
look upon the lake and the mountains beyond. Lacking
no modern convenience, it well deserves the name of
a first-class house. It contains 25 saloons and 250 beds,
ladies' saloon, reading and conversation-rooms, billiard-
room and café-restaurant, dining-hall, and the most modern
hydropathic apparatus; a physician also resides in the house.
The manager is at the same time proprietor of the well-known
Hôtel Paradis at San Remo, in the Riviera, and is famous
for his admirable conduct of his establishments.

Equalling the above, though not in size, yet in every
other respect, and therefore well deserving to be ranked as
first-class houses, are the Hotels *Hof St. Moritz*, *Hornbacher's
Hôtel Engadinerhof*, and — though last, not least — the charming
Hôtel Bellevue with its villas, situated between the Baths of
St. Moritz and the village in a sheltered position, on a gentle
acclivity, and commanding a fine view of the lake and
mountains.

Those who desire to avoid the busier life of the three
larger hotels will find in these three smaller ones somewhat
more seclusion, while at the same time nothing is lacking as
regards convenience of the apartments, saloons, reading-rooms,
etc. etc.

If all these hotels are full, as may chance to happen in
the height of the season, late arrivals can find accommodation
in various snug little *"maisons"* and *"pensions"*, and should
these have all their available space occupied, the last comers
must betake themselves to Campfèr or to the village of St.
Moritz, where several hotels and pensions were built in the
days when little had as yet been done for the accommodation
of visitors at the St. Moritz Baths; from the adjacent villages

invalids drove daily to the springs, not without casting envious glances at the privileged ones who were lodged on the spot.

As to the company frequenting those hotels, it may perhaps interest at least our lady readers to know whom they are likely to meet with here, if only that they may be able to make suitable toilet arrangements.

Turning over the leaves of the visitors' books of St. Moritz Baths and Village, we will select at haphazard a few dozen names of more or less distinguished visitors, as for example: King Charles of Wurtemberg with his consort and the Crown Prince; the Grand Duke and Grand Duchess of Baden, Prince and Princess William of Baden, the Crown Prince of Sweden; the Duchess Wera of Wurtemberg, Duke Philip of Wurtemberg and son; the Prince of Hohenzollern-Sigmaringen; the Grand Duke Louis of Hesse-Darmstadt and the Princess Alice; the Grand Duchess of Mecklenburg-Schwerin; the Grand Duke of Mecklenburg-Schwerin; the Duchess Marie of Mecklenburg-Schwerin (Grand Duchess Wladimir of Russia); the Grand Duke of Oldenburg with consort and son; M. Delbrück.

The Comte de Paris, the Duc d'Aumale and consort, Duc de Guise, Duc de Joinville, Duc de Nemours, Duc de Montpensier, Comte and Comtesse Talleyrand.

King Humbert of Italy, Queen Margaret, and the Crown Prince; and hundreds of noble Italian families (Italy always sends a strong contingent of visitors to St. Moritz).

The Duke of Saxe-Altenburg; the Grand Duchess of Saxe-Weimar.

From Austria: the Grand Dukes Albert, Charles, and Eugene, and the Grand Duchess Gisola. The Prince of Battenberg.

Duke Frederick of Schleswig-Holstein; Princess Henrietta
of Schleswig-Holstein (Frau Geheimrath Prof. Esmarch).

To the above must be added members of the highest
aristocracy of all nations, and the controllers of the money
market: members of the Rothschild families of Frankfort,
Paris, London, Vienna, and Geneva.

Exceeding in number the political potentates are the
intellectual princes and members of the aristocracy of the in-
tellect; of these a brilliant circle assembles every season in
the recreation rooms, and names of world - wide reputation
are not wanting.

But those who have not yet made themselves a name,
or only a modest one, are just as welcome and just as well
cared for — provided only that their hotel bill be punctually
settled — as any prince, whose napoleon contains exactly the
same number of francs as theirs.

It is a matter of course that the proprietors of the
Baths of St. Moritz seek to gain the approval of their distinguished patrons, and make every exertion to maintain, and
if possible to augment, the reputation of this international
health-resort by sparing no expense in the introduction of
improvements of every kind. Of late years great progress
has been made, but much more is intended to be done in
the near future.

A work of great importance is the drainage of the
health-resort on Waring's system, which has everywhere proved
to be the best.

Already in 1868 the communal authorities laid sewer pipes
in the streets of St. Moritz. The considerable gradient at
which they are laid, and the daily periodic flushings, have
not been accompanied with inconveniences of any importance.
For instance, not a single case of typhoid fever has occurred

within the entire district of the health-resort during the last fourteen years.

Nevertheless the management deemed it expedient to satisfy to the full the requirements of modern hygienic science in this respect. The local board of health accordingly commissioned an experienced civil engineer to prepare a plan for the complete reconstruction of the drainage of the place.

The work is being carried out in two separate systems. The rain water, the overflow of the waterwheels, and the underground water are carried off in cemented pipes to natural channels. The sewage, etc., is swept away in continuous pipes to the outlet of the lake, whence it is conducted for a distance of about half a mile through the gorge of the Charnadüra into the Inn. The flow of pure lake water amounts to something like 32,000,000 cubic feet of water in 24 hours, so that in the swiftly-flowing river itself no pollution of any consequence can take place.

The principal hotels have already made connection with this drainage system. A few of the older and smaller houses, mostly frequented by natives, will retain the old arrangements for the present. All houses hereafter to be built must be connected with the drainage system. Both these and the hotels and pensions now standing are bound to fit hermetically-closing cocks and ventilation and vapour pipes between the house pipes and the main pipes, and every new opening must be provided with new cocks and ventilators.

The refuse from houses and stables is regularly disinfected in distant spots.

The materials of the sewer pipes are iron, clay, and stoneware; their minimum fall is 2.5 in 1000. The sewer pipes themselves are from 6 to 10 inches in diameter, so that even when in full use the upper half serves for ventilation, being in connection with proper outlets. Flushing is effected by means of automatically-working basins.

The chief difficulties encountered were the cold of the winter and the rocky foundation of the houses in the village, but both these were successfully overcome.

The expenses of the public sewerage system amounted to nearly £2000, more than half of which sum was covered by voluntary contributions.

It may be mentioned here that since 1876 water is laid on in cast-iron pipes to all the groups of houses. The water has been analysed by professor A. Husemann and found to be of unusual purity.

We have given these details at ¡some length partly on account of the intrinsic importance of the subject, but more especially to show intending visitors that though they are coming into a sequestered valley they will not find themselves among backwoodsmen, but among people who have an exact acquaintance with the requirements of modern civilised life.

Other innovations have also recently been made.

Having regard to the Alpine climate, wood was selected as the material for the bath-tubs first employed. But of late years several complaints were made regarding these somewhat clumsy tubs; it was therefore decided to make a trial of metal baths, and a number of zinc baths of elegant and convenient shape have therefore been introduced. If they meet the approbation of the public they will be immediately introduced throughout in place of the wooden ones. The present method of heating the bath-water by means of injected steam will be continued. For hydropathic purposes, douches on the newest and most approved principles are now provided.

A further improvement deserving mention is that since 1883 the former Carlsbad band of ten performers has been superseded by a Milanese band of sixteen well-trained musicians, who appear to give general satisfaction.

Lastly, by improving the method of lighting, by constructing promenades and paths, and introducing so-called "stradini" for cleansing and watering the roads and walks, the Spa Management have done as much as possible to meet the convenience of their guests.

For the vehicles on hire in the large hotels there is a regular tariff, the Drivers' Union is well disciplined, and elegant and convenient tram-cars stand at the service of visitors to Maloja, Morteratsch, and Samaden.

In the above remarks we have confined ourselves to the exterior of the health-resort, but the interior, that is to say the arrangements directly connected with the medical treatment, are also admirable in every respect. The *therapeutical appliances* likewise leave nothing to be desired as regards completeness.

Owing to the larger amount of iron it contains, the (New) Paracelsus-Quelle is now preferred for *drinking purposes*. The Trinkhalle is comfortably arranged; the water can be warmed in the glasses to the required point, and warm whey is obtainable throughout the forenoon.

The Old Spring yields a copious supply of water, sufficient for from *four to five hundred baths* daily. This bath-water is pumped from the Old Spring into two large reservoirs, whence it flows through pipes into the bath-tubs. Other pipes supply ordinary water for cleansing the tubs, and still others convey the steam used in heating the bath-water. By this method the water is warmed within five minutes to a temperature of from 77 to 86 deg. Fabr., and this rapid heating prevents the escape of any great quantity of the carbonic acid gas, to which these baths owe so much of their efficacy.

The St. Moritz water is exported to the amount of hundreds of thousands of bottles annually, and everything is done in order to insure the retention of its valuable properties.

Medical assistance is abundantly provided for; during the season physicians of the highest eminence are constantly in attendance here.

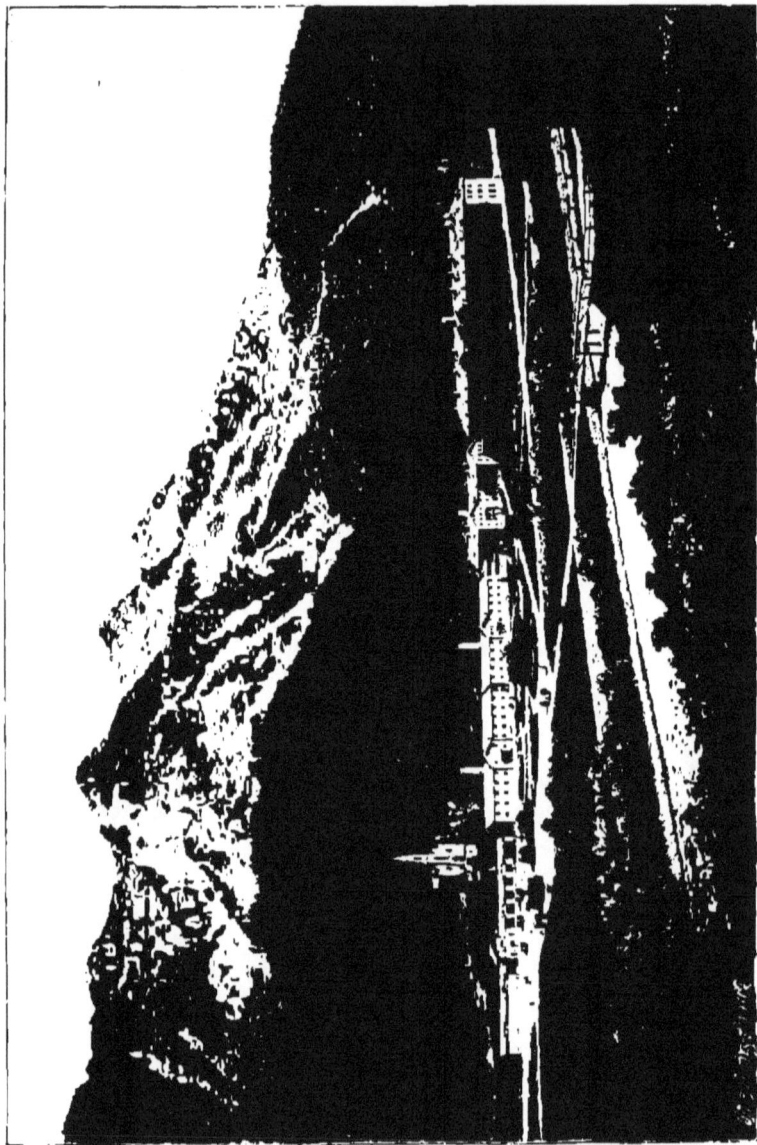

The Kurhaus, Trinkhalle, and French Church.

The Springs.

THE cliff from which the *New Spring*, or *Paracelsus-Quelle*
flows, consists chiefly of granite of the kind found on the
Julier, but a little further up hornblende is mixed with it and
at no great height a transition takes place into fine-grained
syenitic diorite, close to which, however, coarse-grained varieties
of the same stone and also quartziferous syenite and true granite
occur without sharp lines of demarcation.

If no doubt exists as to the origin of the New Spring,
which flows directly from the fine-grained granite, it is on the
contrary a question whether the *Old Spring* originates in the
same formation. When in the year 1853 this spring was newly
enclosed, the old enclosure was found in a very good state
of preservation, and was left with little alteration; it therefore
remains uncertain whether the huge hollowed tree-stem of which
it consists rests upon the rock from which the spring must
originally flow, or only upon the layer of detritus covering the
rock. A point of great importance for the discovery of new
springs therefore remains undecided, namely whether all the
mineral water found here issues from the granite rock or from
the seam between the granite and the crystalline schist above it.

On the wooded southern bank of the Lake of St. Moritz
mica-slate is found, and higher up gneiss, both covered by

deep deposits of peat. The gorge of Charnadüras, in which the River Inn descends from the lake to the second ledge of the valley, is cut through the gneiss. The level ground between the Kurhaus and the lake is composed of detritus and alluvial deposits; nearer to the lake deposits of peat also occur.

Here rises the *third spring,* which was discovered in the autumn of 1864; it could only be followed into the detritus. All attempts to enclose it have hitherto proved unsuccessful. Not far off, in the lake itself, a *fourth spring* is seen to bubble up.

Who was the first to drink of these waters, to experience their healing powers, and to call the attention of others thereto — whether accident played a part here, as tradition assures us it did at so many other springs—of all this we know nothing, although the village of St. Moritz (in *Romansch* San Murezzan) is mentioned in a document as early as the year 1139. In the fifteenth century St. Moritz was known only as a resort of Italian pilgrims. The springs were unenclosed, and ran to waste in the lake. Possibly the first enclosure was made in the time of Paracelsus, who speaks so approvingly of this water, that is to say, in the middle of the sixteenth century. This first enclosure consisted of an enormous hollow larch-stem; in the course of time it became covered up, and was quite forgotten, so that a century later a new enclosure of granite slabs was constructed above it. This we learn from a physician of Milan, Dr. Cesati, who visited the springs in the year 1674; at this time also a roof was first built over them. From this period many Swiss and Italians *) began to frequent the springs, Germans also paid occasional visits, and the chalybeate water was exported to various parts. The spring was in this condition

---

*) In 1697 came Duke Victor Amadeus of Savoy, in 1699 the Duke of Parma, etc.

when visited by the celebrated naturalist and Alpine explorer
J. J. Scheuchzer in the year 1703, but fourteen years later
he was aware that other chalybeate springs existed close at
hand. In 1740 the granite enclosure was renewed, but without
any attempt being made to find the oldest enclosure; a report
was abroad, however, that formerly, when the water flowed
from a tree-stem, the spring was much more powerful: that
after the removal of this stem other water had mingled with
the mineral water and deprived it of its strength. For fear of
losing the entire spring, no further changes were made in the
enclosure until 1853.

During the long years of political strife which followed
the French Revolution St. Moritz and its springs were quite
forgotten, and the place sank from the flourishing condition
which it had reached in 1780. The arrangements for drinking
and bathing, and all the appliances mentioned in the previous
chapter, were of the most miserable kind; the only buildings
were a few tumble-down cottages or rather sheds. Later on
a kind of "saloon" was erected, in which the visitors took
refuge during wet weather, and warmed themselves at the two
stoves. A description of the health-resort in the year 1819
mentions three inns: "the *Lion*, whose landlord, being a butcher,
was able to supply his guests daily with fresh meat, the *Horse*,
which boasted in its landlady a good and cleanly cook, and
lastly the *Eagle*, chiefly frequented by Italians from the
Valtellina."

Many of the visitors appeared at the spring in the morning
on horseback. Where to leave the horse and where to find
temporary lodging was a matter to be decided by each
traveller. Every visitor was expected "to take care of himself."
The commune did nothing at all, and as yet there was no
committee of management. The River Inn too threatened to
overflow and destroy the springs, until in 1815 a new channel

was made for the river, and the impending disaster thereby averted.

In 1830, at the instance of Mr. J. von Flugi, a joint-stock company with £600 capital was formed, which secured from the commune a lease of the springs for 20 years and built a small Kurhaus. This house contained a spa-room and six bath-rooms, but no bed-rooms. St. Moritz sank more and more into forgetfulness.

Its time was not yet come; but soon were to come both the hour and the men.

In 1852 the lease of the old spring expired, and a new commission consisting of the talented physician Dr. Brügger, and of Messrs. von Flugi and L'Orsa began with energy the work of improvement, which embraced the enclosure of the new spring. This was effected in 1853, and, in spite of many difficulties, with complete success. The enterprising trio hereupon gained courage to try and resuscitate the old spring. Something remarkable now happened. On removing the granite enclosure of 1740 and digging deeper, the workmen came to a stratum of earth two feet in thickness, composed of sand, pebbles, and clay mingled with fragments of pottery, coins, and corks, and when this was cleared away the above-mentioned immense larch-stem, together with a smaller one (both hollowed out into the form of barrels) came to light. This then was the original enclosure of the spring, several centuries old, but still in so good a state of preservation that nothing better could be done than to retain it. At the bottom of the "barrel" a leathern bottle was found, dating probably from the sixteenth century. This old enclosure was perhaps covered up in the second half of the sixteenth century. On its rediscovery the spring gained to a remarkable extent not only in quality (common water could no longer dilute it) but also in quantity: previously only two or three quarts per minute had been obtained, but now the spring yields twenty, and if through pumping the water is kept at a low lovel, this quantity can be trebled.

A new company with a larger capital was at once formed. The springs were taken on lease for a term of fifty years; a new Kurhaus was built in 1856, and considerably enlarged ten years later.

From the year 1853, then, dates the renewed prosperity of the health-resort and its world-wide fame, which will no doubt be maintained even if the efforts to enclose the two or three remaining springs should prove, as hitherto, unsuccessful.

The mineral springs of St. Moritz are chalybeate waters containing soda; chemically there is but little difference between the various springs, though the New Spring is somewhat the richer in iron, the Old Spring in carbonate of soda.

Numerous *analyses* of the St. Moritz waters have been made; the first, by a chemist of Berne, Morell, dates from the year 1788; the most recent and the best (1873—74) is that of *Professor Husemann*. It is as follows:

I. The Carbonates calculated as Bicarbonates
(in grammes).

Constituents	In 10,000 grammes of water	
	Alte Quelle	Paracelsus-Quelle
Chloride of lithium	0.00848	0.00885
Chloride of sodium	0.43764	0.34683
Bromide of sodium	0.00536	0.00099
Iodide of sodium	0.00013	0.000024
Fluoride of sodium	0.00630	0.01740
Nitrate of soda	0.00333	0.00721
Borate of soda	0.03614	0.05228
Sulphate of soda	3.07415	3.21101
Sulphate of potassium	0.14382	0.14800
Carbonate of soda	1.92465	1.28273
„ of oxide of ammonia	0.02008	0.01750
„ of lime	8.52025	9.04132
„ of strontia	0.00088	0.00092
„ of magnesia	1.29345	1.32686
„ of protoxide of manganese ...	0.03829	0.04043
„ of protoxide of iron	0.23996	0.28020
Hydrated peroxide of iron ...	—	0.06108
Silicic acid	0 40169	0.53445
Phosphoric acid...	0.00156	0.00144
Alumina	0.00050	0.00030
Baryta, cæsium, arsonic, copper, organic matter	traces	traces
Total solid constituents... ...	16.15666	16.37982
Obtained directly	15.76600	16.14200
Half-free and free carbonic acid:		
a. at 0⁰ and 29.92 bar. ...	15009.06 c.c.	15531.60 c.c.
b. at temperature of spring and 24.21 bar.	18916.06 „	19565.05 „
Free carbonic acid:		
a. at 0⁰ and 29.92 bar. ...	12300.10 „	12828.10 „
b. at temperature of spring and 24.21 bar.	15501.90 „	16156.30 „

II. The Carbonates calculated as Bicarbonates
(in grammes).

Bicarbonates	In 10,000 grammes of water	
	Alte Quelle	Paracelsus-Quelle
Bicarbonate of soda...	2.72356	1.81518
„ of oxide of ammonia...	0.02928	0.02552
„ of lime...	12.26916	13.01950
„ of strontia... ...	0.00114	0.00119
„ of magnesia ...	1.97097	2.02188
„ of protoxide of manganese ...	0.05292	0.05588
„ of protoxide of iron	0.33098	0.33646

It is obvious to the most superficial observer that the
water of the Old Spring contains large quantities of carbonic
acid gas, which cause it to bubble and boil, and render the
air in the upper part of the collector unfit for respiration.
By lifting the cover carbonic acid gas can be taken out in
one's hat; it renders itself perceptible by its well-known
prickly irritation of the mucous membrane of the nose. Its
presence in the waters renders them agreeably cooling to
the taste, and slightly astringent. When taken from the
spring the water appears pure and clear, but if allowed to
stand, exposed to the air, it deposits a yellowish sediment,
or "rust." A slight sediment is also deposited by the water
bottled for export.

The effect of the water consists in promoting change of
tissue (but without acting as a laxative) and increasing
diuresis; the appetite increases, the blood is improved, and
the activity of the nerves is increased. The Alpine climate
seconds the effect of the waters.

The result of all observations may be summed up as follows: The curative influences of the springs and of the climate mutually reinforce and supplement each other as in no other health-resort in the world.

As a climatic watering-place St. Moritz is indeed unique. In most cases the full influence of all the therapeutic factors is not even necessary to produce the desired result; the greatest variation in treatment according to the nature of each individual case is practicable, and important therapeutic effects can be produced in different ways.

The *indications* thus become fuller and more complete, the contra-indications more definite. The former comprise: Cases of illness accompanied by atony, weak constitutions, persons in need of rest from overwork, disturbances of nutrition in general and in respect to particular organs, slow development of torpid persons, rickets, scrofula, difficult reconvalescence, above all malarial sickness, recuperation after treatment at other wells, baths, or climatic resorts. Further, deficient development of the lungs, catarrhs, many cases of asthma; simple and complicated anæmia; disturbances of the functions of the nervous system in consequence of its deficient nutrition, as hysteria, hypochondria, sleeplessness, mental over-exertion; chronic gastric and intestinal catarrh, impotence in the male, and lastly various disturbances of menstruation, sterility, vaginal and uterine catarrh, and chronic metritis.

The *contra - indications* are chiefly conditioned by the climate; they include in general all active states of congestion, plethora, feverish course of diseases, such as of rheumatic and specific conditions; advanced tuberculosis, cancer, syphilis. Further, inclination to apoplexy, hypertrophy of the heart, valvular and other defects, atheroma, aneurisms; important emphysema, severe venous stases in the lungs, catarrh in decrepit persons, advanced age accompanied by deficient generation of heat, gastric ulcer, and in certain cases neuralgic affections attributable to active rheumatic complications.

As regards the duration of a course of treatment, it should neither be too brief nor too long. Under many circumstances from three to four weeks will suffice. Where a longer course is necessary it is divided into two periods, and the patient is sent after the first fortnight to the Valtellina or to Chiavenna and Como, remaining in St. Moritz on his return as long as the physician may advise. Frequently a second course of treatment is necessary, and many persons drink the waters annually during a series of years, or in alternate years.

Walks and Excursions.

THE invalid will soon feel himself sufficiently strengthened to follow the tourist in his walks in the environs of St. Moritz, and to accompany him on longer excursions, at least such as are confined to the valley itself, and do not involve the scaling of the circumjacent heights. But here he meets with an unexpected embarrassment: he cannot decide whither to direct his steps first, for the Engadine offers so much that is attractive and well deserving of nearer inspection.

To enter into details regarding all the single points, though not beyond the purpose of this pamphlet, would lead us to exceed our allotted limits of space. Just at the point where the author would wish to give his pen freer play, and to recall pleasant memories of many a delightful excursion, he finds himself compelled to abbreviate to the utmost, and to give a catalogue of dry names instead of a fresh and inviting description of mountains, forests, lakes, and glaciers.

Of course the people of the Engadine have not left nature unimproved in this direction,—we do not mean as regards her wildly romantic charms and the prospects afforded at the goal of the excursion, but only as regards the ways leading to this goal; but to this we think few visitors will be inclined to object, especially such as are accustomed to the well-paved streets of cities, or who prefer to make their excursions as far as possible by carriage or on horseback.

Acla Silva Farm. Piz Nair in the background.

The most popular points of view and excursions are the following:

To the *Acla Silva*, or *Farm*, situated on a gentle grassy slope on the left bank of the lake, and surrounded by pines.

The *Quellenhügel*, reached by a woodland path in half an hour. It commands a charming view of the lake and the surrounding landscape.

The *Crapp Nair*, a projecting rock commanding a view of the entire valley from Maloja to Madulein; two hours' walk.

Ascent of *Piz Rosatsch* (three hours to the summit), for the strong and vigorous only.

The *Johannisberg* (Crapp St. Gian) is one of the finest points of view, and is easy of access.

The *Acla Alpina* (upper and lower), situated upon a green slope between Campfèr and St. Moritz. Here, as everywhere, refreshments are obtainable.

Alp Giop and *Alp Nova* above St. Moritz, and *Alp Laret* above Celerina, affording extensive views over the valley.

Piz Nair (10,039 feet), ascent across Alp Giop in three hours; guide required.

Crestalta, a pleasant "summer inn," reached from the Kurhaus in three-quarters of an hour, and frequently visited on account of the fine prospect it affords.

Sils Maria and *Maloja*, two points best visited by carriage. From Sils Maria a path leads down into the Fexthal, with the Fex Glacier in the background. The heights of the Maloja Pass can be reached by tram-car in two hours. From here good mountain-climbers may visit the lakes of Cavloccio and Longhino.

Samaden, the capital of the Engadine, and *Pontresina*, much frequented by tourists, can be reached conveniently in various ways.

From Pontresina a visit may easily be paid to the *Morteratsch Glacier*, passing the above-mentioned Languard Waterfall, and to the *Rosegthal* with the celebrated *Roseg Glacier*.

A longer excursion is the drive to the *Hotel on the Bernina Pass*, where we are in the immediate vicinity of the *Cambrena Glacier* and can get a peep into the *Val Poschiavo*. Further than this we will not venture at present.

There remains, if we feel ourselves strong enough for it, to crown our excursions by the ascent of *Piz Languard* (lungo guardo = long view); the first half on horseback, the remainder on foot. This mountain, 10,715 feet in height, has been called the Rigi of the Upper Engadine, but it overtops its western rival by several thousand feet. The view from its summit justifies not only its name, but also the great reputation which it has acquired.

Another mountain which will repay the trouble of the ascent is *Piz Padella* (9458 feet); it commands a view of the Lower Engadine.

Piz Ot may be ascended from Samaden in about four hours; it vies with Piz Languard as regards extent of prospect.

The *Bevers-Thal*, a wild Alpine valley with magnificent mountain flora. *Drive* to the ruins of *Guardavall, near Madulein*.

Drive to the interesting villages of *Zuz* and *Scanfs*, at the lower extremity of the Upper Engadine.

The above are some of the excursions best worthy of mention; there are of course numerous others, longer or shorter, which we must leave the traveller to find out for himself. The district is rich in beauties which well repay the trouble of discovery.

Routes of Access.

THE Baths of St. Moritz are situated, like the entire Engadine, almost in the centre of Europe, and are accessible
from the surrounding countries by numerous mountain-passes
crossed by finely-constructed carriage-roads. The authorities of
the Canton of Grisons, rightly estimating the circumstances,
have spared no expense, but have constructed one mountain
highway after another, so that now there are seven available
for traffic, and these will probably be found to meet every
requirement.

Three of these roads open into the Lower Engadine, and
the remaining four provide direct intercourse with the Baths
of St. Moritz. From *Italy* (Milan) there is the following route
through the Bergell:

Maloja-Engadine.

Colico-Chiavenna-Samaden.		Samaden-Chiavenna-Colico.	
Colico *dep.*	1. — p. m.	St.Moritz-Baths *dep.*	5.45 a. m.
and	8. 20 a. m.	and	3. 10 p. m.
Chiavenna *dep.*...	7. — a. m.	Chiavenna *arr* ...	11. 50 a. m.
and	11. 20 p. m.	and	12. 20 a. m.
St.Moritz-Baths *arr.*	3.25 p. m.	Colico *arr.*	2. 20 p. m.
and	7. 15 a. m.	and	2. 50 a. m.

At *Chiavenna* the Swiss diligence service (the best in the
world) begins. The journey from Chiavenna across the Maloja
to the Baths of St. Moritz occupies about 8 hours. Towards

the beginning of July, 1886, the line of railway from Colico to Chiavenna will be opened. The diligence journey across the pass will then require but 5 hours.

Another route from Italy to the Engadine leads from Tirano in the Valtellina (diligence once a day) through the Poschiavo and across the Bernina Pass, and reaches the Baths of St. Moritz in about 9 1/2 hours.

Other routes available for the traveller coming from the north are the Lenz-Albula and Lenz-Julier routes, both starting from Coire, and both about equally long.

Lenz-Albula.

Coire-Bergün-St. Moritz-Baths.	St, Moritz-Baths-Bergün-Coire.
Coire dep. ... ... 6. 30 a. m.	St.Moritz Baths dep. 6. 45 a. m.
St. Moritz Baths arr. 8. — p. m.	Coire arr. ... ... 7. 30 p. m.

Lenz-Julier.

Coire-Tiefenkasten-Samaden.	Samaden-Tiefenkasten-Coire.
Coire dep. ... ... 11. 10 p. m.	St.Moritz Baths dep. 6. 10 a. m.
St. Moritz Baths arr.11. — a. m.	Coire arr. ... ... 4. 30 p. m.

Schyn-Julier.

Coire-Thusis-Samaden.	Samaden-Thusis-Coire.
Coire dep. ... ... 6. — a. m.	St.Moritz Baths dep.11. 20 a.m.
St.Moritz Baths arr. 7. 15 p. m.	Coire arr. ... ... 9. 50 p. m.

Those who are willing to make a detour, and who would like to see Davos and a part of the Lower Engadine, may drive from Landquart railway station through the Prättigau and Davos, and across the beautiful Flüela Pass; in ten hours Süs in the Lower Engadine is reached, and here the traveller can take the Schuls diligence to Samaden.

Those who desire to avoid crossing mountain-passes can now avail themselves of the new and very interesting route

leading through the beautiful Tyrol and the Lower Engadine
to the Baths of St. Moritz.

Express trains run from Paris, Brussels, Cologne, Frankfort, Basle, Zurich, &c., to Landeck Station, on the Arlberg
Railway. From here the Swiss diligence starts twice daily,
conveying passengers in about 15 hours, by the highly interesting Finstermünz Road, along the River Inn, to the Baths
of St. Moritz, without crossing a pass; to break the journey,
a short stay may be made at the famous health-resort of Tarasp-
Schuls, which serves admirably as a kind of halfway-house.

Visitors from the Tyrol have a choice of two other routes,
namely: Innsbruck-Landeck-Nauders, or Botzen-Meran-Nauders
(on the Austrian frontier), and then by the Swiss diligence to
Tarasp-Schuls in 3¼ hours, and thence into the Upper Engadine.

Communications in the Upper Engadine:

St. Moritz Baths-Samaden-Scanfs.

St Moritz Baths *dep.* 12. — p. m.	
Scanfs *arr.* ... ... 2. 20 p. m.	
(Also: Samaden *dep.* 5. 30	
Scanfs *arr.* 6. 50)	

Scanfs-Samaden-St. Moritz Baths.

Scanfs *dep.* ... ... 7. — a. m.	
St. Moritz Baths *arr.* 9. 35 a. m.	

Samaden-Schuls.

St. Moritz Baths *dep.* 5.10 a. m.	
and 12. — noon	
Samaden *dep.* ... 6.10 a. m.	
and 1. — p. m.	
Schuls *arr.* ... ... 11.40 a. m.	
and 6.45 p. m.	

Schuls-Samaden.

Schuls *dep.* ... ... 1.45 p. m.	
and 6. — p. m.	
St. Moritz Baths *arr.* 8.30 p. m.	
and 3.05 p. m.	

On the Lenz-Julier, Lenz-Albula, Schyn-Julier, Maloja-
Engadine, Bernina, and Prättigau-Flüela routes *extra diligences*
can be had. Tariffs and regulations can be seen at the respective offices.

Every traveller by the diligence is allowed 20 pounds luggage free. Extra weight is charged for.

Those who wish to enjoy the scenery, and do not m the cold air, will do well to telegraph to the starting-pl of the diligence for a seat in the coupé, or still better (only in reliable weather) for an outside seat.